3

In loving memory of
Royal H. Durst

Library of Congress Cataloging-in-Publication Data

Haggadah. English & Hebrew. Selections.
  [Hagadah la-yeladim] = A children's Haggadah / by Howard Bogot and Robert Orkand.
    p.   cm.
    ISBN: 0-88123-059-6 (softcover); 0-88123-060-X (hardcover).
1. Haggadot—Texts—Juvenile literature. 2. Seder—Liturgy—
Texts—Juvenile Literature. 3. Judaism—Liturgy—Texts—Juvenile literature.
[1. Seder. 2. Passover. 3. Judaism—Liturgy.]
I. Bogot, Howard. II. Orkand, Robert. III. Title. IV. Title: Passover Haggadah
BM676.76.B64 1993
296.4'87—dc20   93-21340
                                                                                      CIP
                                                                                      AC

Produced at Nostradamus Advertising
by Barry Nostradamus Sher, Wendy Wolf, Warren Wolfsohn and James Legg.
Set in Fairfield, designed by Rudolf Růžička, and Kastel (Davka Corp.).
Illustrations copyright © 1994 by Devis Grebu
Copyright © 1994, 1995 by the Central Conference of American Rabbis
CCAR Press, 192 Lexington Avenue, New York, NY 10016

95 96 97 98 99   2 3 4 5 6 7 8

BEFORE WE BEGIN

Imagine a world without freedom. Many times in history, our Jewish people lived without freedom.

The Haggadah tells the story of one of those times.

The Haggadah tells about how our people were slaves and then became free.

In our Torah, one of the most important ideas is freedom.

Freedom means different things to different people.

Boys and girls who are free have the right to enjoy schools, libraries, playgrounds, movies, birthday parties, baseball and tennis games, and walks in the park.

To the musician, freedom means the right to play all types of music: jazz, opera, folk, country, rock, and classical.

We are free to choose our own hobbies, jobs and way of life. If we are unhappy, we may try to make changes to make our lives better.

A person who is free may say "Yes" even if everyone else is saying "No."

Let us do what our ancestors have done for thousands of years. Let us remember the story of the Exodus from Egypt. Let us link ourselves with all the Jews who came before us. Let us celebrate freedom!

On the table is a seder plate on which the following foods are found:

) Bitter herbs, such
sh root, remind us
ss of slavery in

s

gypt.

Beitsa) In ancient days,
Jewish festivals of Pesach,
t and Sukkot, our
rs would bring an offering
emple to be roasted in
f the holiday. The roasted
inds us of that sacrifice.

זְרוֹעַ (Z'roa) A roasted bone
reminds us of the special lamb
that was brought to the Temple in
Jerusalem on Pesach as an
offering to God.

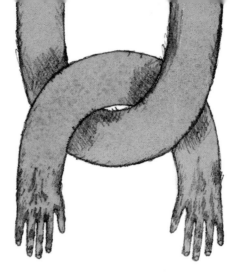

PREPARING FOR THE SEDER

By reading the words of this Haggadah, and by eating special food, we obey the mitzvah written in the Torah: "You shall tell the Pesach (Passover) story to your children in the days to come." The story we tell is how the Jewish people were freed from being slaves in Egypt. We call this the Exodus.

The Torah tells us that Pesach was the first festival that the Jewish people celebrated more than 3000 years ago. They, like us, gathered together in great joy to take part in celebrating the Exodus.

The special meal for Pesach is called the seder. The word 'seder' means 'order.' There is a set order for all the things we do during our seder—things that remind us of the Exodus from Egypt.

ILLUSTRATED AND DESIGNED BY DEVIS GREBU

TEXT BY HOWARD I. BOGOT AND ROBERT J. ORKAND

CENTRAL CONFERENCE OF AMERICAN RABBIS

NEW YORK

we also find:

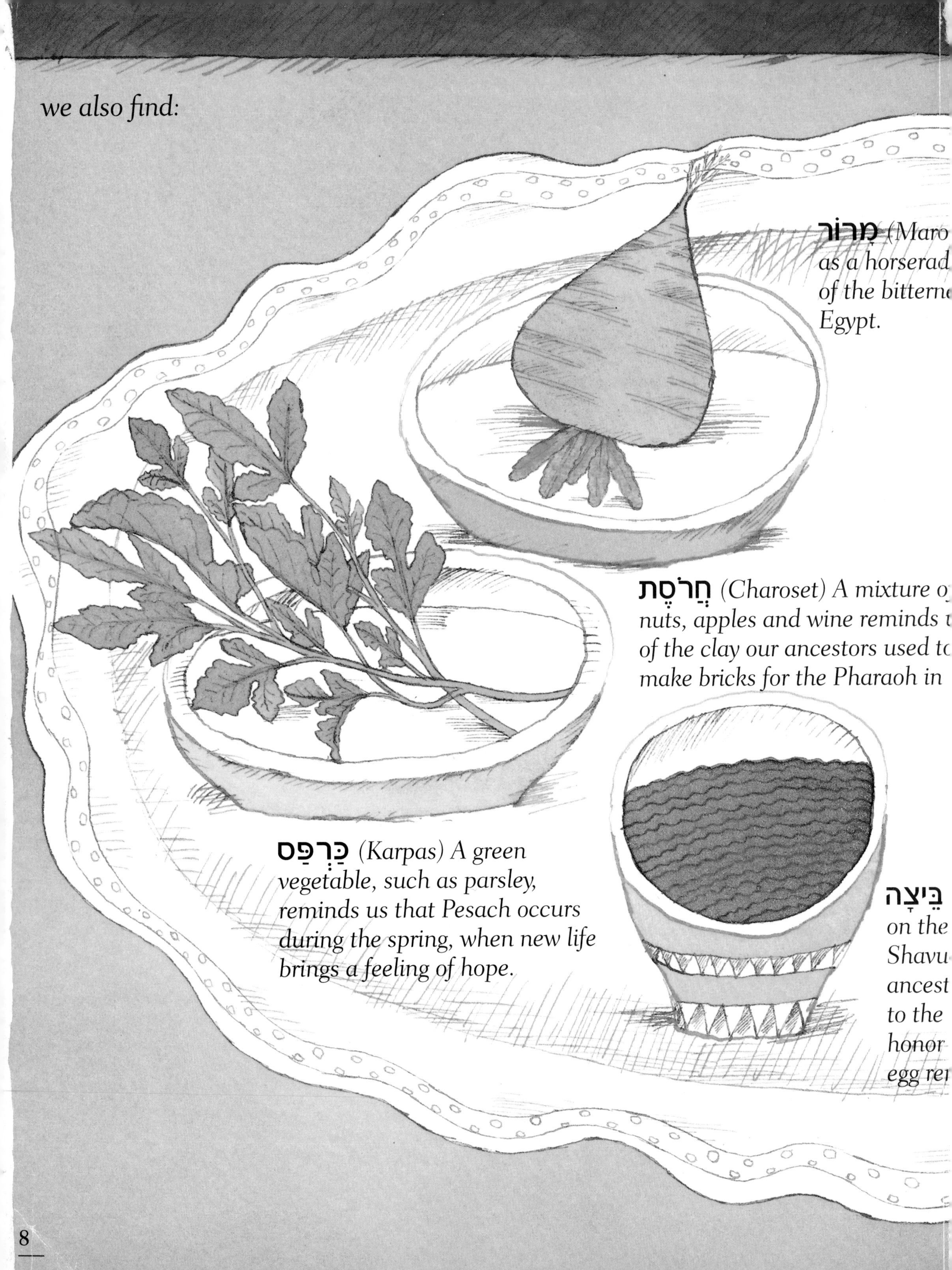

מָרוֹר (Maro...
as a horserad...
of the bitter...
Egypt.

חֲרֹסֶת (Charoset) A mixture o...
nuts, apples and wine reminds ...
of the clay our ancestors used t...
make bricks for the Pharaoh in ...

כַּרְפַּס (Karpas) A green
vegetable, such as parsley,
reminds us that Pesach occurs
during the spring, when new life
brings a feeling of hope.

בֵּיצָה
on the
Shavu...
ancest...
to the
honor...
egg re...

8

מַצָּה (Matzah) Three matzot remind us that there are still three kinds of people: those who are not yet free, those who don't care about the freedom of others, and those who are free and work to help others become free.

On the seder table

יַיִן (Yayin) During the seder meal we drink four cups of wine. They remind us of four of God's promises of freedom for the Jewish people.

מֵי־מֶלַח (Mei-melach) The salt water reminds us of the sad and bitter tears shed by our people when they were slaves, as well as the tears of those who are still not free today. We will dip the karpas in the salt water.

כּוֹס אֵלִיָּהוּ (Kos Eliyahu) We set aside a special cup filled with wine for the prophet Elijah who, we hope, will visit us during the seder. The rabbis of long ago taught that Elijah will come and announce a time when all people will be free.

KADEISH קַדֵּשׁ

BEING HOLY: SANCTIFICATION
As our Pesach holiday begins,
we praise God for our festival of freedom,
a time with family and friends.

הַדְלָקַת הַנֵּרוֹת

LIGHTING
THE FESTIVAL CANDLES

We begin our Pesach seder by lighting the festival
candles.

We praise God who helps us feel special with the
mitzvah to light holiday candles.

(THE CANDLES ARE LIT AS THE BLESSING IS RECITED OR SUNG)

בָּרוּךְ אַתָּה יי אֱלֹהֵינוּ מֶלֶךְ הָעוֹלָם אֲשֶׁר קִדְּשָׁנוּ בְּמִצְוֹתָיו וְצִוָּנוּ לְהַדְלִיק נֵר שֶׁל (שַׁבָּת וְשֶׁל) יוֹם טוֹב.

Baruch ata Adonai Eloheinu Melech ha-olam asher kid'shanu b'mitsvotav v'tsivanu l'hadlik neir shel (Shabbat v'shel) Yom Tov.

We praise You, God, who makes us holy with commandments, so we light the (Shabbat and) holiday candles.

May these candles remind us that we must help and not hurt, cause joy and not sorrow, create and not destroy, and help all to be free.

We praise God for the gift of life and this happy time.

בָּרוּךְ אַתָּה יי אֱלֹהֵינוּ מֶלֶךְ הָעוֹלָם שֶׁהֶחֱיָנוּ וְקִיְּמָנוּ וְהִגִּיעָנוּ לַזְּמַן הַזֶּה.

Baruch ata Adonai Eloheinu Melech ha-olam shehecheyanu v'kiy'manu v'higi-anu laz'man hazeh.

כּוֹס קִדּוּשׁ
KOS KIDDUSH

FIRST CUP OF WINE

In our Pesach story we are told four times,
in different ways, that God promised freedom to
our people. We remember each of those promises
with a cup of wine. With the first cup of wine
we recall the first promise found in the Torah:

"I am Adonai, and I will free you from the
slavery of Egypt."

בָּרוּךְ אַתָּה יי אֱלֹהֵינוּ מֶלֶךְ
הָעוֹלָם בּוֹרֵא פְּרִי הַגָּפֶן:

*Baruch ata Adonai Eloheinu,
Melech ha-olam borei p'ri hagafen.*

We praise You, God, for creating
fruit that grows on the vine.

SPRINGTIME AND SADNESS

וּרְחַץ URCHATZ

We wash our hands.

כַּרְפַּס KARPAS

As we say a blessing and eat a green herb or vegetable, we remember that it was springtime when the Pesach story took place. We dip the greens in salt water to remind us of the tears of our ancestors who suffered cruel slavery. As we taste greens and salt water together, we think about the freshness of spring and the tears of slavery.

(EACH PERSON TAKES SOME GREENS AND DIPS THEM IN SALT WATER.)

בָּרוּךְ אַתָּה יי אֱלֹהֵינוּ מֶלֶךְ הָעוֹלָם בּוֹרֵא פְּרִי הָאֲדָמָה:

Baruch ata Adonai Eloheinu Melech ha-olam borei p'ri ha-adama.

We praise You, God, for creating food that grows from the earth.

YACHATS יַחַץ
A TIME FOR SHARING

Now we break the middle matzah and hide one half for the afikoman. After the meal, we will find the afikoman and everyone will share a taste of it. This reminds us that long ago the special gifts brought to the Temple in Jerusalem were shared. No matter where people live, sharing bread is a way of saying, "You are my friend." It is also a way of sharing what we have with others who may not have as much.

On this night of Pesach
we say to the poor and the hungry:

"Let all who are hungry come and eat." This is the plain bread that our ancestors ate in the land of Egypt. Let all who are hungry come and eat with us. Whoever is in need, come share with us this Pesach seder.

As we celebrate here, we think of Jews everywhere. This year all Jews are not yet free. Let all share with us the hope and freedom of Pesach: next year all shall be free.

QUESTIONS

WHY IS THIS NIGHT DIFFERENT FROM ALL OTHER NIGHTS?

שֶׁבְּכָל הַלֵּילוֹת אָנוּ אוֹכְלִין חָמֵץ וּמַצָּה. הַלַּיְלָה הַזֶּה כֻּלּוֹ מַצָּה:

On all other nights we can eat either leavened bread or matzah, but tonight—only matzah.

שֶׁבְּכָל הַלֵּילוֹת אָנוּ אוֹכְלִין שְׁאָר יְרָקוֹת. הַלַּיְלָה הַזֶּה מָרוֹר:

On all other nights we eat all kinds of vegetables, but tonight we also eat a bitter herb—maror.

Why?

were once slaves in Egypt. God, with great strength, helped us go free.

THE FOUR

מַה נִּשְׁתַּנָּה הַלַּיְלָה הַזֶּה מִכָּל הַלֵּילוֹת?

שֶׁבְּכָל הַלֵּילוֹת אֵין אָנוּ מַטְבִּילִין
אֲפִלוּ פַּעַם אֶחָת.
הַלַּיְלָה הַזֶּה שְׁתֵּי פְעָמִים:

On all other nights we dip one food in another, but tonight we must dip twice. First, we dip karpas in salt water and then we dip maror in charoset.

שֶׁבְּכָל הַלֵּילוֹת אָנוּ אוֹכְלִין בֵּין
יוֹשְׁבִין וּבֵין מְסֻבִּין.
הַלַּיְלָה הַזֶּה כֻּלָּנוּ מְסֻבִּין:

On all other nights we sit straight in our chairs, but tonight, we lean to one side.

This night is different in order to remind us that the Jewish people

Mah Nishtana

Israeli Tune

Intro

Mah nish-ta-na ha - lai - la ha-zeh mi - kol___ ha - lei - lot,   mi -

kol___ ha-lei - lot?

Verse

1. Sheh-b' -chol ha-lei-lot___ a - nu och-lin cha -
2. Sheh-b' -chol ha-lei-lot___ a - nu och-lin sh' -
3. Sheh-b' -chol ha-lei-lot ein a-nu mat-bi-lin a -
4. Sheh-b' -chol ha-lei-lot___ a - nu och-lin bein yosh-

meitz___ u-ma - tza,   cha - meitz___ u-ma - tza   Ha -
ar___ y' - ra - kot   sh' - ar___ y' - ra - kot   Ha -
fi - lu pa-am e - chat,   a - fi - lu pa-am e - chat   Ha -
vin u-vein m'-su - bin.   bein yosh- vin u - vein m'-su - bin.   Ha -

lai - la ha-zeh, ha - lai - la ha-zeh ku - lo___ ma - tza___ Ha -
lai - la ha-zeh, ha - lai - la ha-zeh ku - lo___ ma - ror.___ Ha -
lai - la ha-zeh, ha - lai - la ha-zeh sh' - tei f' a - mim.___ Ha -
lai - la ha-zeh, ha - lai - la ha-zeh ku - la-nu m'-su - bin.___ Ha -

lai - la ha-zeh, ha - lai - la ha-zeh ku - lo___ ma - tza.
lai - la ha-zeh, ha - lai - la ha-zeh ku - lo___ ma - ror.
lai - la ha-zeh, ha - lai - la ha-zeh sh' - tei f' a - mim.
lai - la ha-zeh ha - lai - la ha-zeh ku - la-nu m'-su - bin.

THE FOUR CHILDREN אַרְבַּעַת־הַבָּנִים

When we explain something, we want everyone to understand. This is especially true of the Pesach story and seder. The Torah commands us four times that we must teach children about the Exodus from Egypt. These four commands suggest that there are four kinds of children, each of whom learns in a different way.

The **wise** child says, "I want to know the meaning of all these rules." This child is proud to be a Jew and is interested in sharing experiences that are important to Jews. We answer this child by teaching all the rules of Pesach.

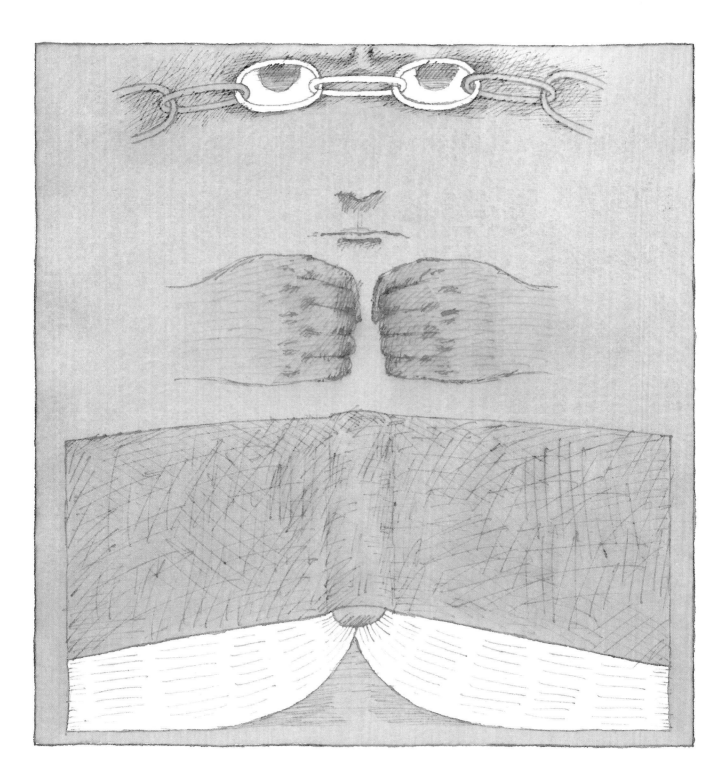

The **wicked** child says, "Why do you bother with all these rules?" This child does not include himself or herself in this question and acts like a stranger when attending a seder. We answer this child by saying, "Had you been in Egypt at the time of the Exodus, you would not have been included when God freed our ancestors from slavery."

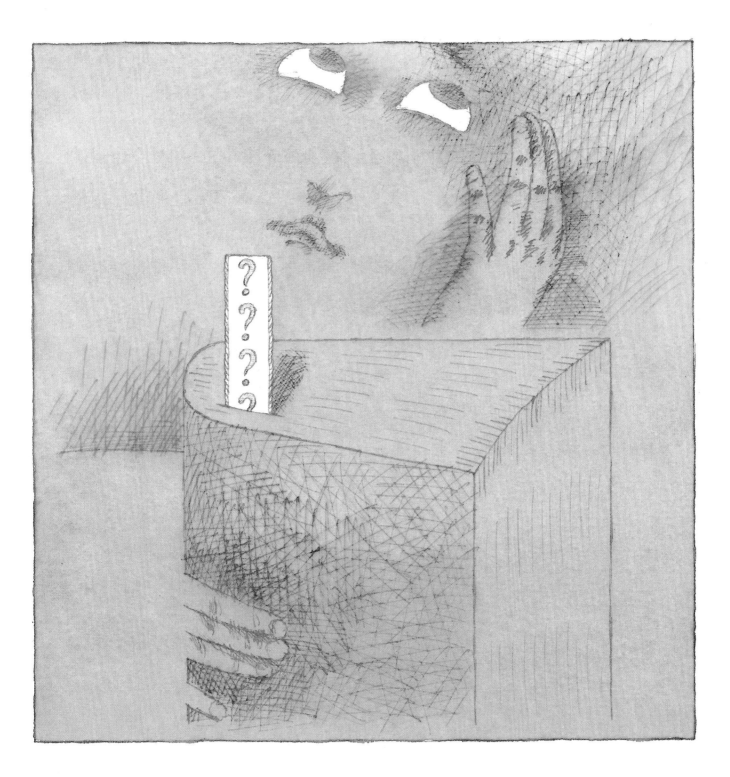

The **simple** child says, "What is this all about?" This child needs to understand basic facts. We answer this child by saying, "We do all these things because God freed us from slavery."

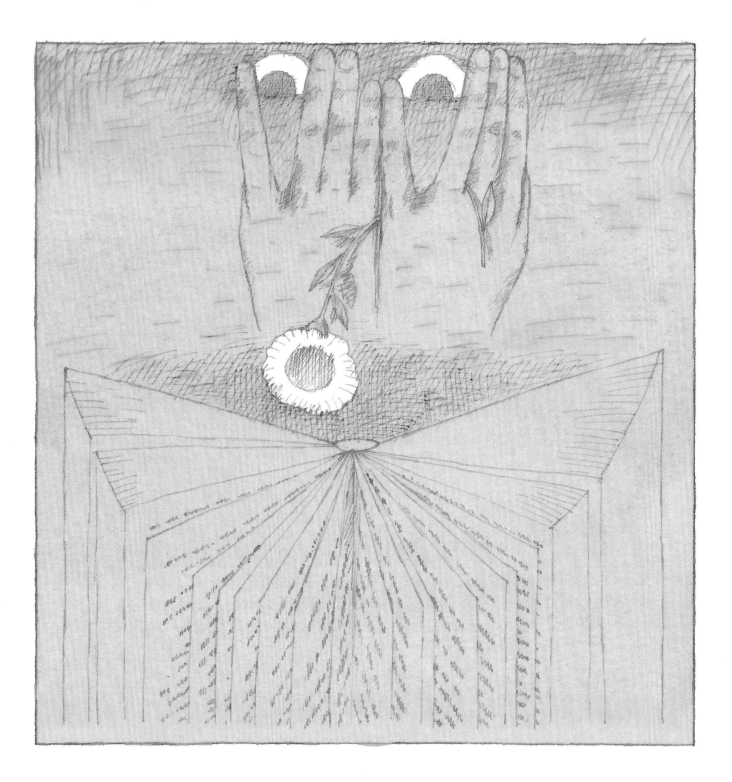

For the child who **does not even know enough to ask,** we explain that "Passover reminds us of what God did for us when we left Egypt." This child needs to learn about Judaism.

MAGGID מַגִּיד
THE STORY

Jewish history began a long time ago.

Our people have lived in many countries. Our people celebrate life in Jewish ways. Throughout Jewish history, angry, frightened and cruel people have wanted to hurt us, but God has given us patience, strength, pride, and hope.

The Jewish people still lives!

It is important to remember how God helps our people survive.

Am Yisraeil Chai

S. Rockoff

Am Yis - ra - eil chai, am Yis - ra - eil chai, am Yis - ra - eil chai.

Am Yis - ra - eil chai, am Yis - ra - eil chai,

1. am Yis - ra - eil chai. 2. am Yis - ra - eil chai. *fine*

Od A - vi - nu od A - vi - nu od A - vi - nu chai, od A - vi - nu od A - vi - nu od A - vi - nu chai,

D.C. al fine

od A - vi - nu od A - vi - nu od A - vi - nu chai, od A - vi - nu chai.

עַם יִשְׂרָאֵל חַי. עוֹד אָבִינוּ חַי.

The Jewish people lives! God, our Parent lives!

This Pesach seder
is our special way
to relive a time
when our people were slaves.
With God's help,
our people became free.

Avadim Hayinu

S. Postolsky

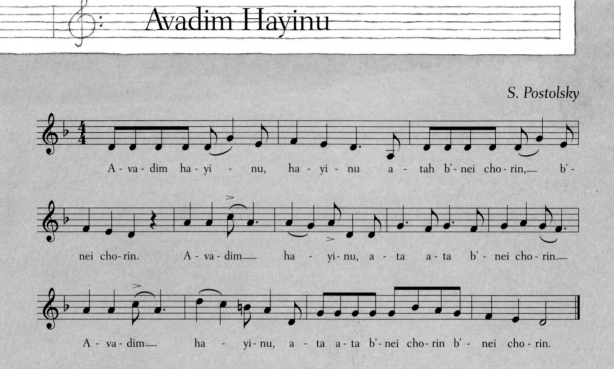

A - va - dim ha - yi - nu, ha - yi - nu a - tah b'- nei cho - rin,— b'-

nei cho - rin. A - va - dim— ha - yi - nu, a - ta a - ta b'- nei cho - rin.—

A - va - dim— ha - yi - nu, a - ta a - ta b'- nei cho - rin b'- nei cho - rin.

עֲבָדִים הָיִינוּ, עַתָּה בְּנֵי חוֹרִין.

Once we were slaves. Today we are free!

29

The Torah tells us that our ancestor Jacob moved with his family from Canaan to the land of Egypt in order to find a better supply of food.

In those days, our ancestors were called Hebrews.

The Hebrews were a small group when they arrived in Egypt.

Jacob's son, Joseph, worked for the Pharaoh, the ruler of Egypt. Joseph's wisdom and skill helped all the people in Egypt. Joseph became an important and respected man. It was the best of times, and the Hebrews grew in number and were happy.

Years passed.

A new Pharaoh, who did not know about Joseph's good deeds, came to power. He was afraid of the large number of Hebrews in his country. He was afraid that the Jewish people would turn against him.

The Pharaoh ordered that the Hebrew people become slaves. They were forced to work day and night to make bricks and build cities. It was a terrible time for the Jewish people!

The Hebrews living in Egypt cried to God.
They wanted to be free!
God heard their cries
and made the Egyptians suffer
with terrible punishments called plagues.

THERE WERE TEN PLAGUES:

**(AS WE ANNOUNCE EACH PLAGUE
WE TAKE A DROP OF WINE FROM OUR CUP
AND PUT IT ON A DISH.)**

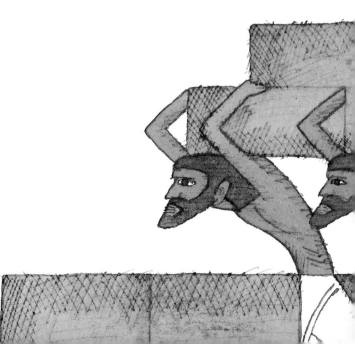

DAM דָּם

There was BLOOD in all the water of Egypt. The Egyptians could not bathe. They could not take a drink. They could not water their flowers or crops. They could not enjoy a refreshing swim.

TS'FARDEI-A צְפַרְדֵּעַ

FROGS hopped and croaked everywhere. No one could sleep, walk or play in peace. The noise was awful! Everything seemed to be moving, and people were dizzy.

KINIM כִּנִּים

LICE made everyone scratch their skin so hard that people hurt all over.

AROV עָרוֹב

WILD BEASTS galloped, slithered, snorted, growled, roared and clawed in every corner of Egypt. Soon, there was no room for the people.

DEVER דֶּבֶר

There were DISEASES that could not be cured. Coughing, sneezing, sore throats, gasping for breath, watering eyes and aching arms and legs made everyone miserable.

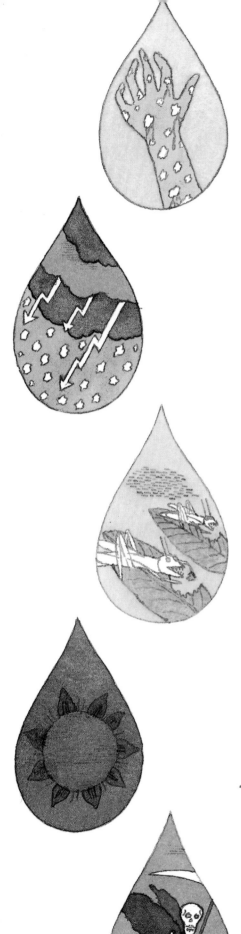

SH'CHIN שְׁחִין

BOILS burst from their skin. They were so uncomfortable! The Egyptians could not even get dressed without screaming from the pain.

BARAD בָּרָד

HAIL rained down as dangerous balls of ice. The hail smashed roofs and damaged crops. It broke everything the Egyptians owned.

ARBEH אַרְבֶּה

LOCUSTS swarmed over all the trees and blades of grass. The buzzing and sound of flapping wings frightened everyone. Vegetables and fruits were gobbled up and only dust remained on the ground.

CHOSHECH חֹשֶׁךְ

DARKNESS blotted out the sun. People were always cold. Moonlight and stars did not appear. Every day was pitch black.

MAKAT B'CHOROT מַכַּת בְּכוֹרוֹת

The first-born son in every Egyptian family DIED.

Finally, the Pharaoh was convinced that the Hebrew people had to be freed from their slavery and he allowed them to leave Egypt.

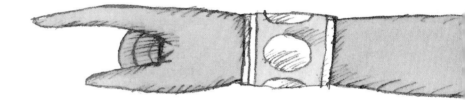

But, after they left Egypt, the Pharaoh changed his mind.

The armies of Egypt were behind them and a great sea was in front of them. The sea held them back, but with God's help the sea parted and our people passed through on dry land.

A new and happy time began for our people. As they stood on the other side of the sea they sang words we still sing today: "Who is like you, Oh God? You are the Eternal One, the One who saved us!"

Pesach is a time to thank God for making our lives and our world better. We are grateful for everything!

If God had only created the world and not brought us out of Egypt, it would have been enough: Dayeinu.

If God had only brought us out of Egypt but not divided the sea: Dayeinu.

If God had only divided the sea but not helped us cross on dry land: Dayeinu.

If God had only helped us cross on dry land but had not given us the Sabbath: Dayeinu.

If God had only given us the Sabbath but had not given us the Torah: Dayeinu.

If God had only given us the Torah but had not sent us wise teachers: Dayeinu.

Dayeinu

Verse

1. I - lu ho - tzi ho - tzi - a - nu, ho - tzi - a - nu mi - mitz - ra - yim,
2. I - lu na - tan, na - tan la - nu, na - tan la - nu et ha - sha - bat,
3. I - lu na - tan, na - tan la - nu, na - tan la - nu et ha - to - rah,

ho - tzi - a - nu mi - mitz - ra - yim da - yei - nu. (to chorus)
na - tan la - nu et ha - sha - bat, da - yei - nu. (to chorus)
na - tan la - nu et ha - to - rah, da - yei - nu. (to chorus)

Chorus

Da - da - yei - nu, ____ da - da - yei - nu, ____ da - da - yei - nu, da -

1.
yei - nu da - yei - nu da - yei - nu.

2. (to next verse)
yei - nu da - yei - nu.

אִלּוּ הוֹצִיאָנוּ מִמִּצְרַיִם. דַּיֵּנוּ׃

אִלּוּ נָתַן לָנוּ אֶת־הַשַּׁבָּת. דַּיֵּנוּ׃

אִלּוּ נָתַן לָנוּ אֶת־הַתּוֹרָה. דַּיֵּנוּ׃

47

We are grateful for everything that God has done for our people.
Tonight we remember how God brought us out of Egypt.
Now is the time to answer the Four Questions.
Now is the time to understand why this night is different.

Why do we eat matzah on Pesach?

Matzah is made with carefully prepared flour mixed with water.
It has no yeast. Matzot are baked until crispy, brown, and flat.
Eating matzah reminds us that when our people—once slaves
in the Land of Egypt—were escaping to freedom, they did not
have time to bake fancy loaves of bread.

This night is different because tonight, at our seder, we eat
matzah instead of bread.

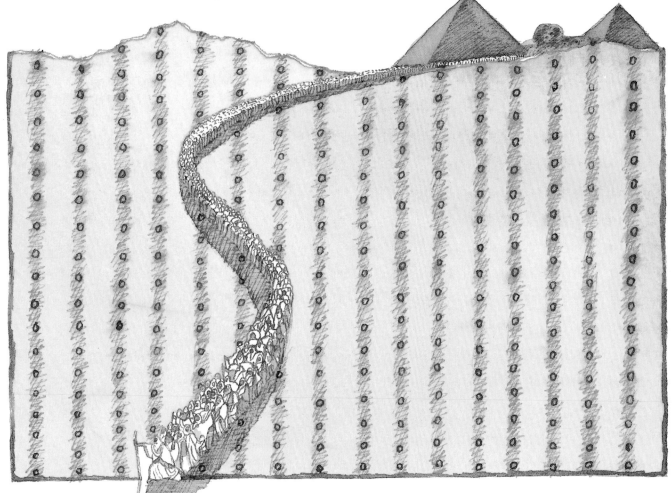

Why do we eat maror at the seder?

Maror is the bitter herb on our seder plate.

Maror reminds us that the Egyptians made the lives of our ancestors bitter when they were slaves. Each year, as we sit together at the seder table, we imagine that each of us went out of Egypt. The Torah teaches us: "And you shall explain to your child on that day, it is because of what God did for me when I, myself, went out of Egypt."

49

Why do we dip foods twice?

We dip karpas
in salt water
to remind us
of the tears
our people cried.

We dip the maror
in the charoset
to remind us
that the Jewish slaves
worked very hard
in Egypt.

Charoset is the sweet mixture on the seder plate. It looks like the clay our ancestors used to make the bricks for the Pharaoh. When we combine something bitter with something sweet, we remember that even when people are sad there is always hope for a happier time.

Why do we lean in our chairs at the seder?

Long ago, free people could lean on a pillow during meals to relax and be comfortable while slaves served them food. We lean on a pillow to remind ourselves that once we were slaves but now we are free.

כּוֹס גְּאוּלָה
KOS G'ULA

With this second cup of wine we remember the second promise God made to the Jewish people: "I will deliver you from their slavery."

We learn that people should not make other people slaves.

God wants us to be free.

בָּרוּךְ אַתָּה יי אֱלֹהֵינוּ מֶלֶךְ הָעוֹלָם בּוֹרֵא פְּרִי הַגָּפֶן:

Baruch ata Adonai Eloheinu Melech ha-olam borei p'ri hagafen.

We praise You, God, for creating fruit that grows on the vine.

EATING THE PESACH FOODS

We understand the meaning of our Pesach foods. Now we are ready to eat them. First, the matzah:

(THE UPPERMOST OF THE THREE MATZOT IS BROKEN AND DISTRIBUTED AMONG THE GROUP)

בָּרוּךְ אַתָּה יי אֱלֹהֵינוּ מֶלֶךְ הָעוֹלָם הַמוֹצִיא לֶחֶם מִן הָאָרֶץ:

Baruch ata Adonai Eloheinu Melech ha-olam hamotsi lechem min ha-arets.

We praise You, God, for bread.

בָּרוּךְ אַתָּה יי אֱלֹהֵינוּ מֶלֶךְ הָעוֹלָם אֲשֶׁר קִדְּשָׁנוּ בְּמִצְוֹתָיו וְצִוָּנוּ עַל אֲכִילַת מַצָּה:

Baruch ata Adonai Eloheinu Melech ha-olam asher kid'shanu b'mitsvotav v'tsivanu al achilat matzah.

We praise You, God, for the commandment to eat matzah.

We now put some maror on a piece of matzah and say a blessing:

בָּרוּךְ אַתָּה יי אֱלֹהֵינוּ מֶלֶךְ הָעוֹלָם אֲשֶׁר קִדְּשָׁנוּ בְּמִצְוֹתָיו וְצִוָּנוּ עַל אֲכִילַת מָרוֹר:

Baruch ata Adonai Eloheinu Melech ha-olam asher kid'shanu b'mitsvotav v'tsivanu al achilat maror.

We praise You, God, for the commandment to eat maror.

Tonight we remember that even though **we** are free, there are still people who are not yet free. Hillel, a famous rabbi of long ago, taught us to eat a special sandwich of matzah, maror, and charoset. By doing so, we put together the matzah of freedom and the maror and charoset of slavery. When people are not free, there is always the hope of freedom.

(MAROR AND CHAROSET ARE EATEN BETWEEN TWO PIECES OF MATZAH.)

שֻׁלְחָן עוֹרֵךְ
DINNER IS SERVED

TSAFUN צָפוּן
THE SEARCH FOR THE HIDDEN MATZAH

Toward the end of the meal, children search
for the hidden afikoman because before we
finish our seder, the afikoman must be found.
Everyone must eat a piece of it.

Tasting matzah as the seder dessert reminds us that
this meal is different.

BAREICH בָּרֵךְ
GIVING THANKS FOR WHAT WE HAVE EATEN

We thank God for rainbows, wisdom, and special times. After every meal we thank God for the food we have eaten. Our prayer is Birkat ha-Mazon.

בָּרוּךְ אַתָּה יי הַזָּן אֶת־הַכֹּל:

Baruch ata Adonai hazan et-hakol.

We praise You, God, in whose world there is food for every person.

We thank God for the strength of the Jewish people. We pray that God will always bless the Jewish people with peace.

Adonai Oz

Psalm 29:11

Ray Cook

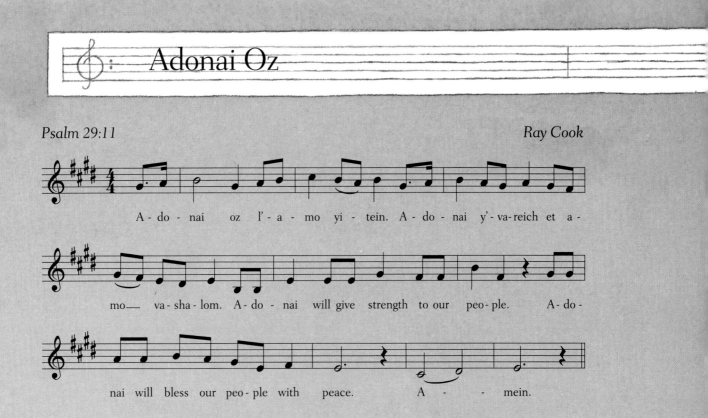

A - do - nai oz l' - a - mo yi - tein. A - do - nai y' - va - reich et a -

mo— va - sha - lom. A - do - nai will give strength to our peo - ple. A - do -

nai will bless our peo - ple with peace. A - - mein.

יי עז לְעַמּוֹ יִתֵּן, יי יְבָרֵךְ אֶת־עַמּוֹ בַשָּׁלוֹם:

כּוֹס בְּרָכָה
KOS B'RACHA

With this third cup of wine we remember the third promise God made to the Jewish people: "I will redeem you with an outstretched arm."

This means that God reaches out to us.

בָּרוּךְ אַתָּה יי אֱלֹהֵינוּ מֶלֶךְ הָעוֹלָם בּוֹרֵא פְּרִי הַגָּפֶן:

Baruch ata Adonai Eloheinu Melech ha-olam borei p'ri hagafen.

We praise You, God, for creating fruit that grows on the vine.

KOS EILIYAHU

THE CUP OF ELIJAH

כּוֹס אֵלִיָּהוּ

There is an extra cup of wine on our seder table that is filled to the brim: "Elijah's Cup." When the prophet Elijah comes he will announce a time when all people in the world will be free. Each of us must help make the prophet's words come true.

We open a door to the outside and hope that Elijah will come now. May these words of the Bible come true tonight:

"Behold, I will send you Elijah the prophet, who will turn the hearts of the parents to the children and the hearts of the children to the parents before the coming of the great and mighty Day of God!" (MALACHI 3:23–24)

(A CHILD OR CHILDREN ARE SENT TO OPEN A DOOR TO THE OUTSIDE.)

Eiliyahu Hanavi

Folk Song

Ei - li - ya - hu ha - na - vi, Ei - li - ya - hu ha - tish - bi, Ei - li - ya - hu, Ei - li - ya - hu, Ei - li - ya - hu ha - gi - la - di. Bim' - hei - ra v' - ya - mei - nu ya - vo ei - lei - nu im ma - shi - ach ben da - vid, im ma - shi - ach ben da - vid.

אֵלִיָּהוּ הַנָּבִיא

אֵלִיָּהוּ הַתִּשְׁבִּי

אֵלִיָּהוּ, אֵלִיָּהוּ, אֵלִיָּהוּ הַגִּלְעָדִי

בִּמְהֵרָה בְיָמֵינוּ יָבֹא אֵלֵינוּ

עִם מָשִׁיחַ בֶּן דָּוִד, עִם מָשִׁיחַ בֶּן דָּוִד.

(Elijah the prophet, in Elijah we will rejoice, may the day come quickly, when the Messiah will come, the descendant of King David.)

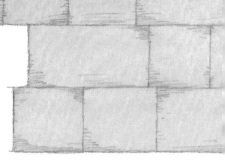

HALLEIL הַלֵּל

PSALMS OF PRAISE

Halleluyah! We say words of praise to God. We sing songs and say words written in the days when the Temple stood in Jerusalem.

We praise God for nature.	HALLELUYAH!
We praise God for truth.	HALLELUYAH!
We praise God for safety.	HALLELUYAH!
We praise God for freedom!	HALLELUYAH!

Hal'luya

Psalm 113

Ha - l'- lu - ya ha - l'- lu - ya ha - l'- lu av - dei a - do - nai.

Ha - l'- lu - ya ha - l'- lu - ya ha - l'- lu et sheim a - do - nai.

Ha - l'- lu - ya, ha - l'- lu - ya, ha - l'- lu - ya, ha - l'- lu - ya.

Let all that live sing prais - es to God. Ha - l'- lu - ya.

הַלְלוּיָהּ הַלְלוּ עַבְדֵי יי הַלְלוּ אֶת־שֵׁם יי׃

כּוֹס הַרְצָאָה
KOS HARTSA-A

THE FOURTH CUP

Our seder is almost over. We lift our cups for
the last time. With this fourth cup of wine we
remember the fourth promise to the Jewish people:
"And I will take you to be my people."
We learn that God loves us.

בָּרוּךְ אַתָּה יי אֱלֹהֵינוּ מֶלֶךְ
הָעוֹלָם בּוֹרֵא פְּרִי הַגָּפֶן:

*Baruch ata Adonai Eloheinu Melech
ha-olam borei p'ri hagafen.*

*We praise You, God, for creating fruit
that grows on the vine.*

Our seder is now ending. We have said special words and have eaten different foods. We know that once we were slaves but now we are free. Not all people are free. There are people who are hungry. On this Pesach night we promise to help all people who are hungry and in need.

May there be
freedom and peace
for us!
For everyone!

This is our hope:

לְשָׁנָה הַבָּאָה בִּירוּשָׁלָיִם

L'shana haba-a bi-Y'rushalayim!

NEXT YEAR IN JERUSALEM! NEXT YEAR, MAY ALL BE FREE!

L'shana Haba-a

L' - sha - na ha - ba - a bi' - y'ru - sha - la - yim, l' - sha -
na ha - ba - a___ bi' - y'ru - sha - la - yim, l' - sha - na ha - ba - a___ bi' -
y'ru - sha - la - yim, l' - sha - na ha - ba - a bi' - y'ru - sha - la - yim.

PESACH SONGS

Chad Gadya

Intro

Chad gad - ya___ chad gad - ya___

Chorus

di - z' - van a - ba bit - rei___ zu - zei.

Chad gad - ya,___ chad gad - ya___

Verse

1. V' - a - ta shun - ra v' - a - chal l' - gad - ya.
2. V' - a - ta kal - ba v' - na - shach l' - shun - ra
3. V' - a - ta chu - tra v' - hi - ka l' - kal - ba

A *　　　　　　　　　**B ***　　　　　　　**To Chorus**

(omit for verse 1 -)
ent a - chal l' - gad - ya.___ (omit for verse 2 - - - - - - - - - - - - - - - -)
d' - no shach l' - shun - ra___ d' - a - chal l' - gad - ya.___

***Alternately add phrase A and B for subsequent verses.**

4. V'a-ta nu-ra v'sa-raf l'chu-tra.
   d'hi-ka l'chal-ba d'na-shach l'shun-ra.
   d'a-chal l'gad-ya (chorus)

5. V'a-ta ma-ya v'cha-va l'nu-ra.
   d'sa-raf l'chu-tra d'hi-ka l'chal-ba.
   d'na-shach l'shun-ra
   d'a-chal l'gad-ya. (chorus)

6. V'a-ta to-ra v'sha-ta l'ma-ya.
   d'cha-va l'nu-ra d'sa-raf l'chu-tra.
   d'hi-ka l'chal-ba d'na-shach l'shun-ra.
   d'a-chal l'gadya (chorus)

7. V'a-ta ha-sho-cheit v'sha-chat l'to-ra.
   d'sha-ta l'ma-ya d'cha-va l'nu-ra.
   d'sa-raf l'chu-tra d'hi-ka l'chal-ba.
   d'na-shach, l'shun-ra
   d'a-chal l'gad-ya. (chorus)

8. V'a-ta mal-ach ha-ma-vet
   v'sha-chat la-sho-cheit.
   d'sha-chat l'to-ra d'sha-ta l'ma-ya.
   d'cha-va l'nu-ra d'sa-raf l'chu-tra.
   d'hi-ka l'chal-ba d'na-shach l'shun-ra.
   d'a-chal l'gad-ya (chorus).

9. V'a-ta ha-ka-dosh ba-ruch Hu
   v'sha-chat l'mal-ach ha-ma-vet
   d'sha-chat la-sho-cheit.
   d'sha-chat l'to-ra d'sha-ta l'ma-ya.
   d'cha-va l'nu-ra d'sa-raf l'chu-tra.
   d'hi-ka l'chal-ba d'na-shach l'shun-ra.
   d'a-chal l'gad-ya (chorus).

(My father bought for two zuzim an only kid . . . Then came the Holy One, blessed be God, and destroyed the angel of death, that slew the butcher, that killed the ox, that drank the water, that quenched the fire, that burned the stick, that beat the dog, that bit the cat, that ate the kid.)

Echad Mi Yodei'a

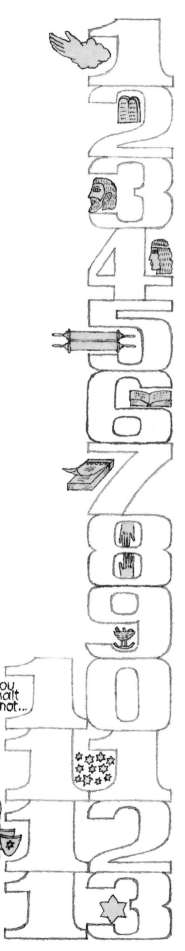

Folk Song

1. Eh - chad mi yo - dei - a? Eh - chad a - ni yo - dei - a!
2. Sh'na - yim mi yo - dei - a? Sh'na - yim a - ni yo - dei - a!

Repeat as needed

(Omit for first verse -)
Sh'nei lu - chot ha - brit___

Eh - chad Eh - lo - hei - nu sheh - ba - sha ma - yim u - va - a - retz!
Eh - chad Eh - lo - hei - nu sheh - ba - sha ma - yim u - va - a - retz!

3. Sh'-lo-sha mi yo-dei-ah?
   Sh'-lo-sha a-ni yo-dei-ah.
   Sh'lo-sha a-vot. Sh'nei lu-chot ha-brit. Eh-chad Eh-lo-hei-nu sheh-ba-sha ma-yim u-va-a-retz!

4. Ar'bah mi yo-dei'a?
   Ar'bah a-ni yo-dei'a.
   Ar'bah i-ma-hot. *(etc.)*

5. Cha-mi-sha mi yo-dei'a?
   Cha-mi-sha a-ni yo-dei'a.
   Cha-mi-sha chum-shei to-rah. *(etc.)*

6. Shi-sha mi yo-dei'a?
   Shi-sha a-ni yo-dei'a.
   Shi-sha sid-rei mish-na. *(etc.)*

7. Shi-va mi yo-dei'a?
   Shi-va a-ni yo-dei'a.
   Shi-va y'mei shab-ta. *(etc.)*

8. Sh'mo-na mi yo-dei'a?
   Sh'mo-na a-ni yo-dei'a.
   Sh'mo-na y'mei mi-lah. *(etc.)*

9. Ti-sha mi yo-dei'a?
   Ti-sha a-ni yo-dei'a.
   Ti-sha yar-chei lei-dah. *(etc.)*

10. A-sa-rah mi yo-dei'a?
    A-sa-rah a-ni yo-dei'a.
    A-sa-rah dib'ra-yah. *(etc.)*

11. A-chad a-sar mi yo-dei'a?
    A-chad a-sar a-ni yo-dei'a.
    A-chad a-sar ko-va-yah. *(etc.)*

12. Sh'neim a-sar mi yo-dei'a?
    Sh'neim a-sar a-ni yo-dei'a.
    Sh'neim a-sar shiv-ta-yah. *(etc.)*

13. Sh'lo-sha a-sar mi yo-dei-ah?
    Sh'lo-sha a-sar a-ni yo-dei-ah.
    Sh'lo-sha a-sar mi-da-yah. *(etc.)*

[Beginning with verse 4, sing the bold words and the bold words of all previous verses.]

(Who knows one? I know one. One is our God in heaven and earth. Two are the tables of the commandments. Three is the number of the patriarchs. Four is the number of the matriarchs. Five books there are in the Torah. Six sections the Mishnah has. Seven days there are in a week. Eight are the days to the service of the covenant. Nine are the months to bear a child. Ten commandments were given on Sinai. Eleven were the stars in Joseph's dream. Twelve are the tribes of Israel. Thirteen are the attributes of God.)

Adir Hu

(Hebrew verses 2–4
begin here)

A - dir hu   a - dir hu yiv -
God of Might,   God of Right,

neh vei - to b' - ka - rov   bim - hei - ra
We would bow be - fore You, Sing Your praise

bim - hei - ra b' - ya - mei - nu b' - ka - rov
in these days, Cel - e - brate Your glo - ry,

Eil b' - nei eil b' - nei b'nei veit - cha b' - ka - rov.
As we hear, year by year, Free - dom's won - drous sto - ry:

2. Ba-ḥur hu, ga-dol hu, da-gul hu . . .
3. Na-or hu, sa-giv hu, iz-uz hu . . .
4. Po-deh hu, tsa-dik hu, ka-dosh hu . . .

2. How God gave to each slave
Promised liberation,
This great word Pharaoh heard
Making proclamation:
Set them free to serve Me
As a holy nation.

3. We enslaved thus were saved
Through God's might appearing,
So we pray for the day
When we shall be hearing
Freedom's call reaching all,
The people's God revering.

Pesach is Here Today

Words and Music by Steven Carr Reuben

1. Pe - sach is here to - day. The Se - der is on its
2. What's on a Se - der plate?___ Tell me, I just can't
3. This is a spe - cial night,___ Ev - 'ry - thing must be

way. All of the fam' - ly gath - ers to - geth - er,
wait. Ma - tza's af - flic - tion, mar - ror is bit - ter,
right. Clean the cha - meitz from all of the cup - boards,

thoughts of free - dom bring - ing. Pha - roah en - slaved us,
sweet - ness is cha - ro - set; Kar - pas is spring - time,
Search in ev - 'ry cor - ner. Cook spe - cial foods and

then Mo - ses saved us, And we went out sing - ing.
Ya - yin we drink wine, Shank - bone is z' - ro - a.
then set the ta - ble. Ev - 'ry - thing's in or - der.

Lai lai lai lai lai lai lai lai lai lai lai lai lai lai lai

lai lai lai lai lai lai lai lai lai lai lai lai lai lai lai.

Kadeish Ur'chatz

Malcolm H. Stern

Babylonian Melody

1. Ka - deish—— u - r' - chatz—— ka - r' - pas—— ya - chatz.
2. Praise God for fruit of vine, and you may drink one cup of wine.
3. Ma - tza you bless and eat. With bit - ter herbs, cha - ro - set sweet.

Ma - gid—— ra - cha - tza—— mo - tzi—— ma - tza.
In salt you dip some green. Break the ma - tza in be - tween.
At last the meal takes place. But be - fore you say the grace,

Ma - ror—— ko - reich shul - chan—— o - reich.
Of three ma - tzot on the tray, take one piece to hide a - way.
Find the a - fi - ko - man. Bring the sup - per to its end.

Tza - fun—— ba - rech ha - lel—— nir - tza.
Read how God set Is - ra - el free, res - cued us from sla - ve - ry.
Then re - cite the psalms of praise, fi - nal thanks to God we raise.

Go Down, Moses!

Spiritual

When Is - rael was in E - gypt land, "Let my peo - ple

go!" Op - pressed so hard they could not stand, "Let my peo - ple go!"

Go down, Mo - ses, Way down in E - gypt land,——

Tell— old Pha - raoh "Let my peo - ple go!"

72

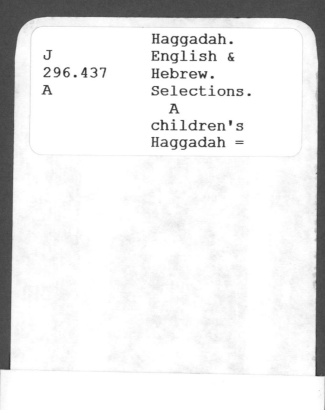